RIDING IN THE SWEET LIGHT
Quotes by Jim Hicks

Copyright © 2024 by Jim Hicks
ISBN: 979-8-9893547-1-9

ALL RIGHTS RESERVED. No part of this book may be reproduced or transmitted in any form by any means, electronic or mechanical, including photocopying and recording, or by any information storage and retrieval system, except as may be expressly permitted in writing from the publisher. Requests for permission should be addressed to Eclectic Horseman Comm. Inc. Attn: Rights and Permissions, P.O. Box 174, Elbert, CO 80106.

All interior photos by Donnette Hicks **sagecreekequestrian.com** and Kim Stone **shinanatu.com**.

Layout and Design by Emily Kitching.

www.eclectic-horseman.com

TABLE OF CONTENTS

Foreword iv

Introduction vi

The Quotes 1

Afterword 103

FOREWORD

Reflecting on my forty year journey with horses, I recognize the pivotal influence of Ray Hunt. His teachings have been profound in my life. They have highlighted my desire to constantly learn from the horse. Recognizing threshold moments in my journey signifies a deep moment of transformation—when past experiences converge with new insights, leading to a shift in perspective. These moments have redefined my relationship with horses and have opened new avenues for understanding, connection, and communication. With every Ray Hunt clinic, Ray would often say "think." What that meant for me was when I am doing something and it isn't working, to think and do something different. Followed by observing, evaluating and reaching for balance.

My journey has been full of relearning what is possible by reflecting the essence of growth in any of my endeavors. It speaks to the inquisitive nature of knowledge and experience that sometimes stepping back and reassessing what we think we know can lead to breakthrough moments. This is often when real learning occurs—when we let go of preconceived notions and welcome new perspectives.

Exceptional horsemanship is an indicator of the rider's ability to control their emotional energy. It's the desire to see things from the horse's perspective and it's the willingness to adjust their feel for the situation as many times as necessary. Each ride and interaction offers new lessons, allowing both horse and rider to evolve together.

The relationship between horse and rider transcends mere technical skill; it becomes a dance of trust, awareness, and shared experience. Embracing these principles not only enhances abilities but also celebrates the horses wisdom.

Surrendering oneself to moments of achieving a sense of stillness allows for genuine connection. True horsemanship is a lifelong journey of self-discovery, learning, and humility.

It's clear that my relationship with horses is multifaceted. Such a journey illustrates a lifelong commitment to learning and evolving in the art of horsemanship.

"There is a very sacred feeling inside, which guides me with vulnerability. It's when I am able to remove my humanity and become quiet. It's where I surrender to the breath of the horse."

-Jim Hicks

INTRODUCTION

A Partnership Like No Other Thanks to Jim Hicks

I always say that I knew I wanted a horse before I was born. People smile and many actually nod in agreement. But it's true.

I grew up with Roy Rogers and Trigger, Annie Oakley and Target, and Gene Autry and Champion, and they all confirmed my commitment to achieving that dream someday.

I reveled in the way their horses galloped up and down hills in pursuit of the "bad guys" and stood still when their riders dismounted and walked away. But I never gave any thought to what exactly was going on between the horse and rider to make all of this happen. It never occurred to me that any kind of preparation was necessary to effectively achieve the results of the ride and the response of the horse. After all, isn't that what horses were designed to do?

It took me 33 years to acquire my first horse and that's when a personal and profound journey began. Finding my way with an animal that was big, athletic, sentient, and honest came with a huge learning curve and a deep commitment to do my best with a gift that was like no other.

But it wasn't until I found my way to Jim Hicks that the clarity and effectiveness began to come together. It was with Jim that I began to realize what good horsemanship really meant and how it was the foundation for building trust, respect, and being effective with my horses. Like learning a new dance with a partner, Jim taught me to keep it simple. Warming up for our lesson was an opportunity to check in with the basics: Is there energy, rhythm? What about flexion? Is there lateral bend, alignment, and connection? Bingo! He helped me to be mindful about feel and timing, and knowing where the feet are. And to be diligent about recognizing even the slightest change, because if it's effective, it's understood.

And so our journey continues. Thank you, Jim for being a mentor, a dear friend, and another gift that is like no other.

Happy Trails!
Lynn de Freitas

"What horsemanship means to me is the ability to overcome myself in order to feel what the horse needs."

"Discipline your thinking, discover your feel, connect in lightness."

"When we humanize the horse, we lose connection to its nature."

"New insights about horses can be discovered with a simple exchange of thoughts and ideas between friends ."

"My responsibility is to recognize the unique qualities of each horse and cultivate a masterpiece accordingly."

"The horse will reflect the rider's inauthenticities."

"In any relationship there are two points of view. One is not more valuable than the other. The challenge is to find the equilibrium between the two sets of needs. When the balance of emotional and physical needs are met the horse and rider can harmonize."

"I hear people label a horse as counterfeit. I have not observed a counterfeit horse. I have witnessed the horse being honest about the riders ability or lack of ability."

"When you offer good feel, all there is to do is trust the process."

"Even when we don't understand, nature works in perfect order."

"You will need to wait a little longer to be a part of the miracle."

"Horses carry far more of our human pain than we are willing to face."

"When the leg and hand compliment each other, the rider is able to develop higher degrees of balance for the horse."

"Stop duplicating someone else's steps, find your own path."

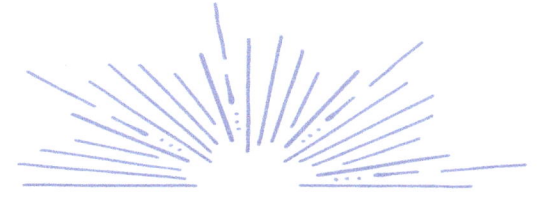

"The rider needs to develop a thoughtful approach in the training. The goal should be to create a soundness of the mind and body."

"Small challenges, overcome daily, lead to big confidence later."

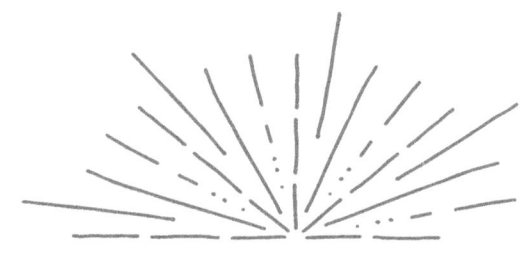

"Consistency is where progress happens."

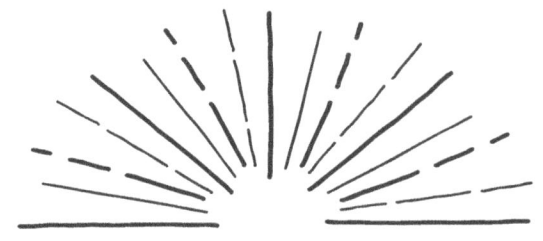

"The rider that is habitually stuck in the loop of overthinking the ride, will miss the opportunity to develop the necessary feel and timing in the present moment."

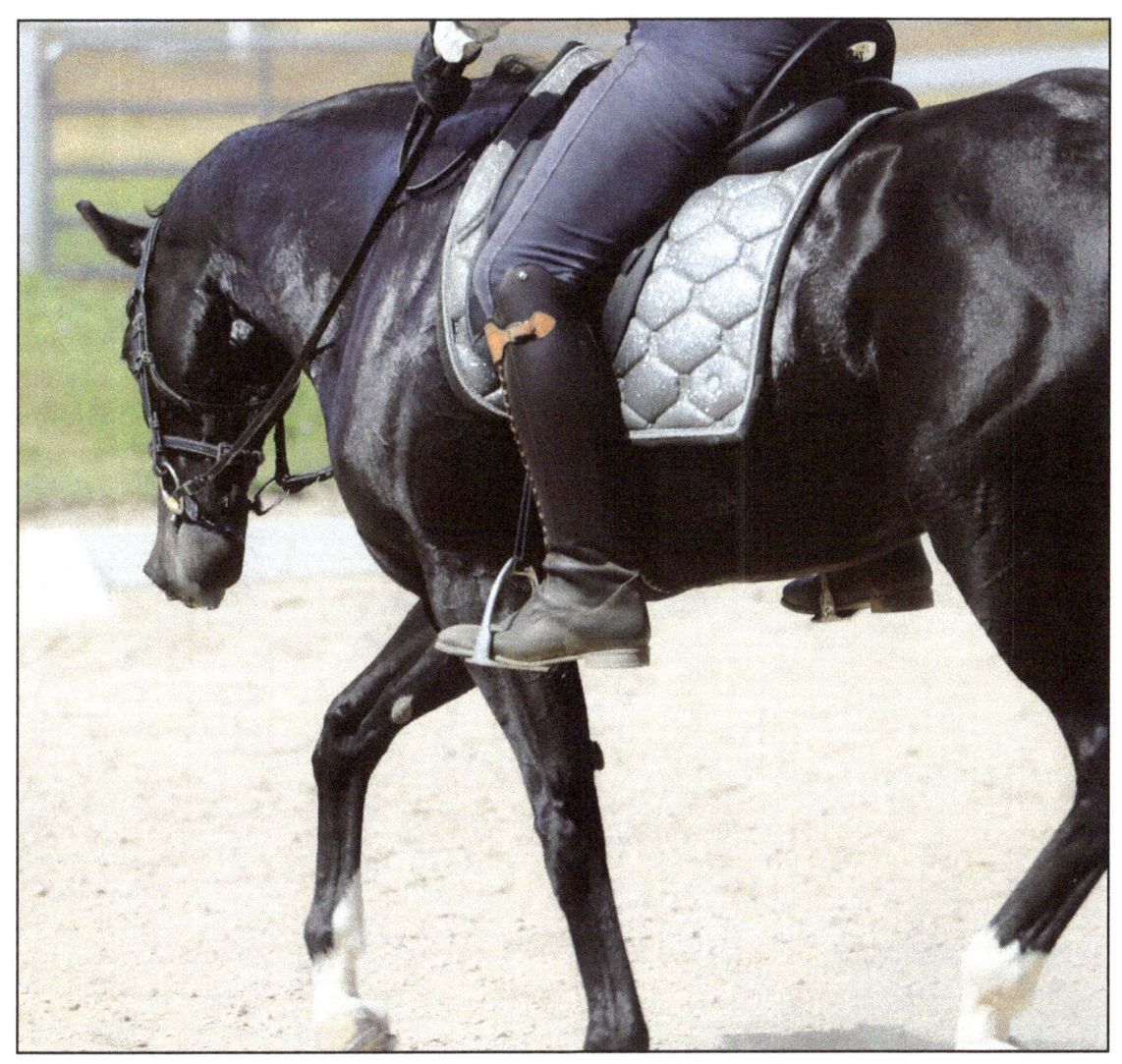

"Each day is a new opportunity to reflect on what you have to offer the horse."

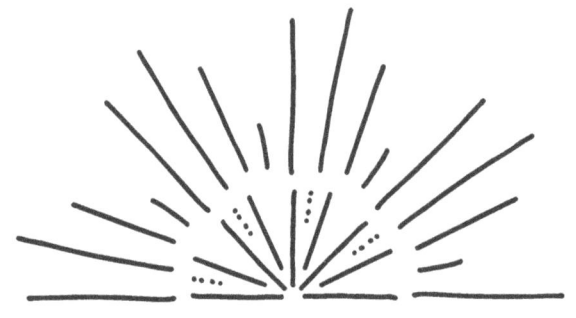

"The rider that can evaluate progress or or lack of progress honestly, can make the necessary adjustments to empower the horse."

"The other side of bad feel and timing is good feel and timing."

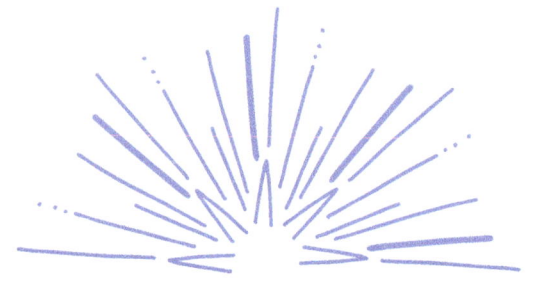

"If what you are offering the horse is not working, what do you have to lose by doing something different?"

"Be here now. That is what horsemanship means to me."

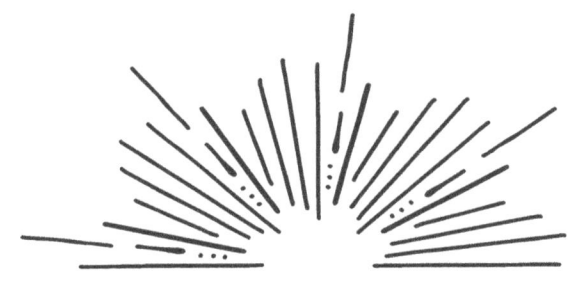

"There is no other place or time more valuable than now."

"Horsemanship is not easy, you have to earn it. You learn it through a lot of soul searching and commitment."

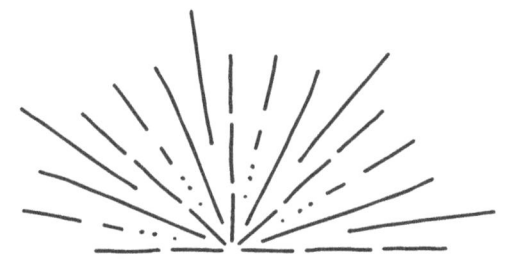

"A willingness to move into the unknown is where you will find the answers."

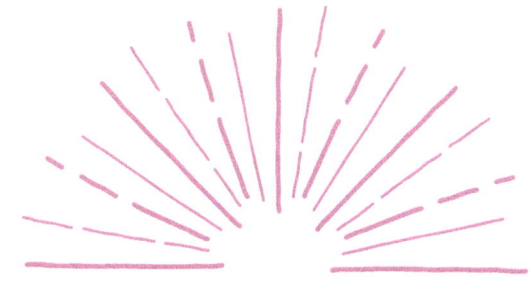

"I see unique potential in each horse."

"I don't expect the horse to be who they are not."

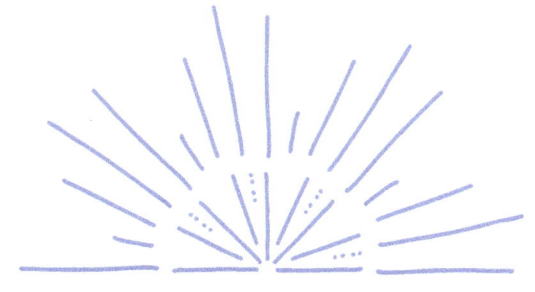

"The rider that becomes critical in their attitude and approach will miss what the horse has to offer."

"The rider that can adapt the attitude of being clear in communication with the horse, enhances the horses ability to learn with ease."

"I admire the horse's ability to forgive the shortcomings of the human."

"Don't mistake humility for the lack of ability."

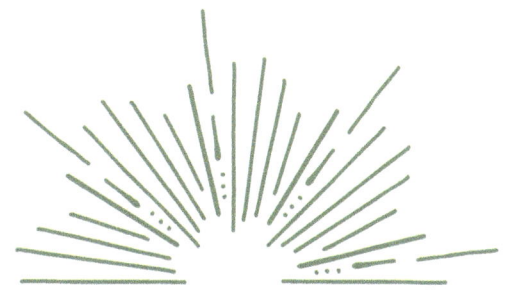

"I hear riders talk about connection, and their interpretation is what happens between their hands to the mouth through the reins. For me it starts with a mental connection which begins the moment I step into their presence."

"Exceptional horsemanship begins with an awareness of what is working and what is not working, and knowing the difference."

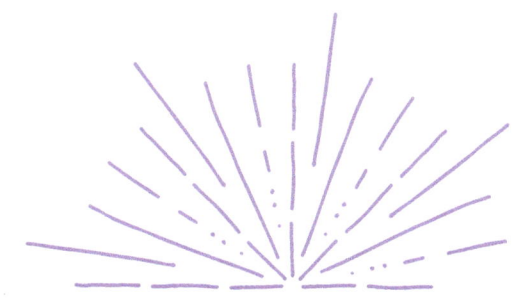

"When you are not communicating well with the horse, double check the basics, confirming the horse has the necessary tools to answer the question powerfully."

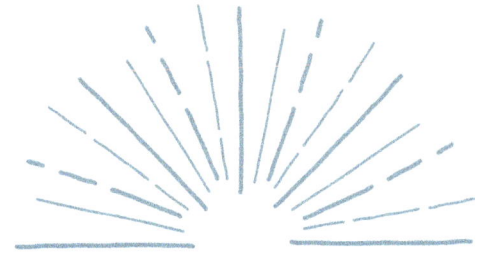

"The rider has a responsibility to keep moving the education forward in a productive way."

"The horse is often confused by the rider's inconsistent feel and timing."

"The rider needs to become aware of their energy and how it affects the horse's ability to respond confidently."

"There is what the horse needs from me. There is what I need from the horse. Then there's what is needed from both sides: a partnership of mutual understanding."

"As long as the rider wants to place blame, justify, make excuses, they will not develop the potential of the horse."

"Horsemanship is the willingness to take complete responsibility for what the horse does or does not understand."

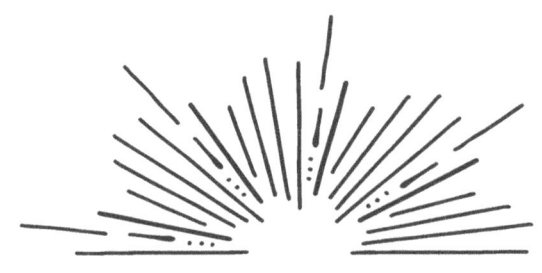

"The horse does not have a voice. They communicate through body language and expression. The rider has a responsibility to recognize and understand what is being communicated."

"Feel and timing is like a heartbeat- it never stops."

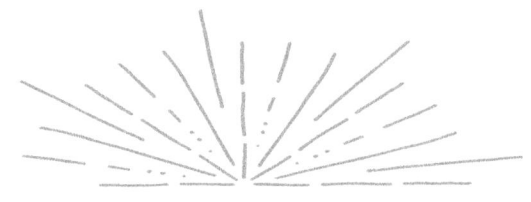

"The rider that chooses to go to war with the horse will lose. When you learn to work with the nature of the horse anything is possible."

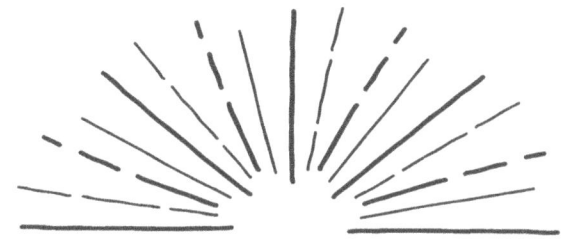

"The rider that is disciplined in their thoughts and actions will improve the quality of communication."

"Horsemanship is the ability to redirect anxiety into relief."

"How the rider presents the feel from their hand to the horse's mouth is going to develop concern or confidence, either way the responsibility is in your hands."

"Good habits create safety. Good habits and safety enhances the rider's ability to calculate risk."

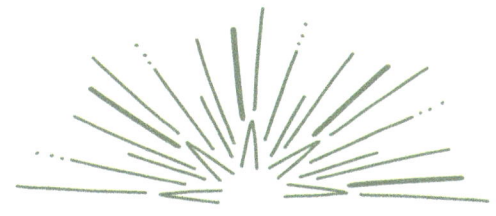

"The horse is not obligated to accommodate the rider who is unwilling to learn."

"Are you aware of your energy and how it affects the horse's state of mind?"

"Offer the horse a feel that inspires trust."

"Amazing moments of horsemanship occur when the horse and rider become harmonious in thought and action, resulting in synchronization."

"The horse is not responsible for the rider's feelings, however the rider is responsible for how the horse feels about what is being communicated."

AFTERWORD

The creation of this book has allowed me to ruminate over my relationship with horses. For me my sensitivity to the horse, hinges on what I am willing to receive as the horse reflects who I am. Developing self knowledge gives me a larger access of how I affect the horse with my choices. I am a committed student of the horse who is open to constantly shifting, changing and growing. The breed of horse, discipline or the tack that they are in does not factor. Every horse encounter is an opportunity to gather insights and experiences. Whether I am starting a colt, out in the mountains or in the show ring, maintaining a mindset of curiosity and openness enriches the journey and connection with the horse.

I take pride witnessing humans succeed in authentically working with their horse. The learning never ends in the equestrian world. Every horse encounter is an opportunity to gather insights and experiences. A good teacher cultivates a space where students feel safe to express themselves and grow. I feel an outstanding coach is committed to their own development, seeking opportunities to learn and expand their knowledge about horsemanship. This commitment to lifelong learning sets a powerful example.

My desire with this book is to create a simple language of quotes for readers to ponder a ardent response in their horsemanship journey.

- Jim Hicks, October 2024

www.ingramcontent.com/pod-product-compliance
Lightning Source LLC
Chambersburg PA
CBHW061942130526
44582CB00042B/92